Miracles

Kaal Bhairav Mandir is a Hindu temple located in the city of Varanasi, Uttar Pradesh, India. It is dedicated to Lord Kaal Bhairav, who is considered to be a fierce form of Lord Shiva. The temple is one of the most important and popular shrines in Varanasi, and it attracts a large number of devotees every day.

The temple has a unique architectural style, and it is built in the traditional North Indian style of temple architecture. The main deity of the temple, Lord Kaal Bhairav, is depicted

with eight arms, holding various weapons and symbols of power.
The temple is also known for its unique rituals and customs, and it is believed that Lord Kaal Bhairav grants the wishes of his devotees who visit the temple with a pure heart and offer their prayers with devotion. Overall, Kaal Bhairav Mandir is a significant pilgrimage destination for Hindu devotees, and it is revered as a powerful spiritual center that embodies the divine presence of Lord Kaal Bhairav.

INDEX

Chapter- 1

who is kaal bhairav

Kaal Bhairav is a Hindu deity who is regarded as a fierce form of Lord Shiva, one of the principal deities of Hinduism. In Hindu mythology, Kaal Bhairav is believed to be the lord of time and a protector of devotees.

The name "Kaal Bhairav" is derived from two Sanskrit words, "kaal" meaning time and "bhairav" referring to a form of Lord Shiva. As such, Kaal Bhairav is often depicted as a ferocious-looking deity with a black complexion, wearing a garland of skulls around his neck and carrying a trident, drum, and sword.

KAAL BHAIRAV

The word Bhairav is a combined form of the words
Bha = creation, Ra = sustenance, Va =
destruction(defining the combined nature of
Brahma, Vishnu ,and Mahesh respectively).

Chapter- 2
history of behind kaal bhairav

The history of Kaal Bhairav dates back to ancient Hindu mythology. According to the Puranas, Kaal Bhairav was created by Lord Shiva in response to Lord Brahma's arrogance. Brahma had become too proud of his powers and started boasting about his abilities, leading Lord Shiva to create a fierce deity to punish him.

As per the legend, Kaal Bhairav was given the task of beheading one of Lord Brahma's heads as a punishment for his arrogance. After executing his task, Kaal Bhairav wandered the earth, carrying the skull of Brahma's head as a reminder of the consequences of pride and arrogance.

The story tell that a conversation broke out between Lord Vishnu & Brahma questioning who is supreme amongst the three of them: Brahma-the creator, Vishnu-the sustainer, and Shiva-the distroyer. A pillar of light erupted from the earth and asked them to find out its end. Both Brahma & Vishnu started their search for the end of the Prakash Stambh (the pillar of light / Jyotirlinga). Eventually, Vishnu surrendered to the ultimate reality but Brahma failed to do so. Yet Brahma didn't accept his defeat and started the show of his authority. The act of Brahma made Shiva angry which resulted in the origin of the fierce form of Rudra from his hair lock when he plucked it and threw it on mighty Mandrachal.

Mighty Shiva ordered Bhairav to punish Brahma by cutting his fifth head from which he uttered the insults to Shiva. Following the order , the fierce kaal Bhairav cut away the 5th head of Brahma with his little fingernail. The Brahma's head got stuck to the Bhairav's nail and now the curse of Brahma Hatya followed him. Worried Bhairav roamed around the universe to get rid of Brahma Hatya but not even the holiest of holy tirth helped him. At the suggestion of Lord Vishnu, Kaal Bhairav entered the city of light : Kashi, where on the bank Matsyodari Tirtha (present Macchodari) and Ganga the kapal (Head) of Brahma fell on earth, hence both Brahma & Kaal Bhairav got liberated and Brahma Hatya moved to pataal . Following it, kaal Bhairav took his penance at the sangam of matsyodari tirth & Ganga which became famous as Kapal Mochan Tirtha. Shiva pronounced the Kaal Bhairva will remain in Kashi in order to remove sins of the disciple and punishment giver before the liberation of souls after which Shiva will give Taraka Mantra for Moksha.

Over time, Kaal Bhairav came to be worshipped as a protector and destroyer of evil forces. It is believed that he possesses the power to dispel fear and anxiety and can protect his devotees from negative energies and spirits.

The Kaal Bhairav Mandir in Varanasi, India, is one of the most significant shrines dedicated to Lord Kaal Bhairav. The temple's origins are not entirely clear, but it is believed to have been built during the Mughal era.

The temple's significance lies in its unique rituals and customs, which are believed to be an essential aspect of worshiping Kaal Bhairav. Devotees offer prayers and perform aarti to the deity with reverence and devotion, seeking his blessings for protection and success.

Overall, the history of Kaal Bhairav is closely intertwined with the legends and mythology of

Hinduism. He is a powerful deity who is revered for his ability to protect and destroy, and his worship is considered an important means of seeking spiritual guidance and overcoming obstacles in life.

Punishing Brahma

Chapter- 3
Introduction to the Kaal Bhairav Temple in Varanasi

The Kaal Bhairav Temple is a renowned Hindu temple located in the holy city of Varanasi in India. It is dedicated to Lord Kaal Bhairav, who is believed to be an incarnation of Lord Shiva. The temple is situated near the Dashashwamedh Ghat and is considered to be one of the most significant temples in Varanasi.

The temple is named after the fierce form of Lord Shiva, Kaal Bhairav, who is depicted as the guardian of the city of Varanasi. The deity is worshipped by devotees who seek protection and blessings. The temple is believed to have been constructed by the Maratha ruler, Maharaja Ranjit Singh, in the 18th century.

The architecture of the temple is unique and impressive, with its black stone structure and intricate carvings. The entrance of the temple is adorned with the trident and the Damru, which are symbols of Lord Shiva. The temple also has a courtyard and a sanctum where the idol of Kaal Bhairav is enshrined.

The temple is visited by thousands of devotees every day, especially on Tuesdays and Sundays, which are considered auspicious days for worshipping Lord Kaal Bhairav. The temple is also known for its tantric rituals and practices, which are performed by the priests to appease the deity.

In conclusion, the Kaal Bhairav Temple is a significant place of worship for Hindus and is renowned for its unique architecture and tantric practices. It is a must-visit destination for anyone visiting the holy city of Varanasi.

Apart from its religious and cultural significance, the Kaal Bhairav Temple is also a popular tourist attraction. Visitors can witness the daily aarti (prayer ceremony) and seek blessings from the deity. The temple complex also has a small market where devotees can purchase offerings for the deity.

The temple is located in close proximity to other important landmarks in Varanasi, such as the Kashi Vishwanath Temple and the Dashashwamedh Ghat. This makes it a convenient destination for tourists who are exploring the city.

However, visitors must also be aware of the temple's strict rules and regulations. Non-Hindus are not allowed to enter the inner sanctum of the temple, and photography is strictly prohibited. Visitors must also dress modestly and remove their shoes before entering the temple complex.

In conclusion, the Kaal Bhairav Temple is not just a place of worship, but also a cultural and architectural marvel. Its significance in Hinduism and its unique practices make it a must-visit destination for anyone interested in exploring the religious and cultural heritage of India.

The temple is also known for its annual festival, which is celebrated with great enthusiasm by the devotees. The festival, called Kaal Bhairav

Ashtami, is celebrated on the eighth day of the Hindu month of Kartik (October-November). On this day, the idol of Lord Kaal Bhairav is taken out in a procession, and devotees offer prayers and seek blessings from the deity.

The Kaal Bhairav Temple is not just a spiritual destination, but also an important landmark in the history of Varanasi. It has been visited by several prominent personalities, including the former Indian Prime Minister, Indira Gandhi.

The temple is open to visitors from 5 am to 9 pm every day, and there is no entry fee. However, visitors are encouraged to make a donation towards the maintenance of the temple and its facilities.

In conclusion, the Kaal Bhairav Temple is a significant place of worship that attracts both devotees and tourists. Its unique architecture, cultural practices, and religious significance make it a must-visit destination in Varanasi. Visitors can experience the spirituality and cultural heritage of India in this magnificent temple dedicated to Lord Kaal Bhairav.

The Kaal Bhairav Temple is also known for its association with the ancient Indian practice of tantra, which involves the use of rituals, mantras, and meditation to attain spiritual enlightenment.

The priests at the temple are well-versed in these practices and perform various tantric rituals to appease the deity and seek his blessings.

The temple complex also has several shrines dedicated to other Hindu deities, including Lord Ganesha, Lord Hanuman, and Goddess Durga. These shrines are popular among devotees who seek blessings from these deities.

The temple's location near the Dashashwamedh Ghat makes it a convenient destination for tourists who wish to take part in the evening Ganga Aarti, a ritual where priests offer prayers and light lamps to the River Ganges. The Ganga Aarti is a mesmerizing spectacle and attracts thousands of visitors every day.

Apart from its religious and cultural significance, the Kaal Bhairav Temple is also a center of learning. The priests at the temple offer courses in Hindu philosophy, meditation, and tantra to interested students. This makes the temple a hub of intellectual and spiritual activity.

In conclusion, the Kaal Bhairav Temple is a multifaceted destination that offers something for everyone. Its spiritual significance, cultural practices, and association with tantra make it a must-visit destination in Varanasi. Visitors can witness the rich cultural heritage of India and attain spiritual enlightenment in this magnificent temple dedicated to Lord Kaal Bhairav.

The Kaal Bhairav Temple has also been associated with various legends and stories that add to its mystique. One such legend states that the temple was originally built by Lord Brahma, the creator of the universe, and was later restored by Lord Vishnu, the preserver of the universe.

Another popular legend associated with the temple is that it is the abode of the Navagrahas, the nine celestial bodies in Hindu astrology. It is believed that worshipping Lord Kaal Bhairav at this temple can pacify the malefic effects of these celestial bodies and bring good luck and prosperity.

The temple's location in Varanasi, one of the oldest inhabited cities in the world, adds to its historical significance. Varanasi is considered to be the spiritual capital of India and is renowned for its cultural and religious heritage. The city is also a hub of academic activity and is home to several renowned universities and research institutes.

In conclusion, the Kaal Bhairav Temple is not just a place of worship but also a center of history, spirituality, and learning. Its legends and stories, along with its cultural and religious practices, make it a unique destination that offers visitors a glimpse into the rich heritage of India. A visit to the temple is a must for anyone interested in exploring the spiritual and cultural roots of this ancient land.

Visitors to the Kaal Bhairav Temple can also explore the nearby attractions that make Varanasi a popular tourist destination. The city is home to several other important temples, including the Kashi Vishwanath Temple, one of the twelve Jyotirlingas (divine abodes of Lord Shiva) in India. The city is also renowned for its silk saris, handcrafted goods, and mouth-watering street food.

The Kaal Bhairav Temple is located in the heart of the city and is easily accessible by public transport. Visitors can take a taxi, auto-rickshaw, or local bus to reach the temple. The temple also provides accommodation for devotees who wish to stay overnight and participate in the various rituals and ceremonies.

In recent years, the temple has undergone several renovations and restoration projects to preserve its historical and cultural significance. The authorities have also taken steps to improve the facilities for visitors and ensure their safety and comfort.

In conclusion, the Kaal Bhairav Temple in Varanasi is a magnificent destination that offers visitors a unique blend of history, spirituality, and culture. Its association with tantra, legends, and stories, along with its location in one of the oldest inhabited cities in the world, make it a must-visit destination for anyone interested in exploring the cultural and spiritual heritage of India.

The Kaal Bhairav Temple also plays an important role in the social and economic life of the local community. The temple provides employment to several people, including priests, cooks, and other staff. The temple also supports local businesses, such as shops and restaurants, that cater to the needs of devotees and tourists.

The temple authorities also engage in various philanthropic activities, such as providing education and healthcare services to the underprivileged sections of society. The temple runs several charitable institutions that cater to the needs of the poor and needy.

The Kaal Bhairav Temple is not just a place of worship but also a symbol of India's rich cultural heritage and spiritual legacy. It is a destination that inspires visitors to explore the deeper meaning of life and seek a higher purpose. A visit to the temple is a transformative experience that leaves a lasting impact on the mind and soul.

In conclusion, the Kaal Bhairav Temple in Varanasi is a destination that offers visitors a unique blend of history, spirituality, culture, and social responsibility. Its association with tantra, legends, and stories, along with its social and economic impact, make it a must-visit destination for anyone who wishes to explore the cultural and spiritual roots of India.

The Kaal Bhairav Temple is also a symbol of religious tolerance and unity in India. The temple is open to people of all faiths and beliefs, and visitors are welcomed with open arms. The temple authorities strive to promote harmony and understanding among different communities and foster a spirit of brotherhood and cooperation.

The temple also serves as a venue for various cultural and religious events throughout the year. These events showcase the rich diversity of India's cultural heritage and provide a platform for artists, musicians, and performers to showcase their talent.

The Kaal Bhairav Temple is a living embodiment of India's age-old traditions and customs. It is a destination that connects visitors with the timeless wisdom of the past and inspires them to seek a better future. A visit to the temple is not just a journey of the body but also a journey of the mind and soul.

In conclusion, the Kaal Bhairav Temple in Varanasi is a destination that offers visitors a unique blend of spirituality, culture, social responsibility, religious tolerance, and unity. It is a place that inspires visitors to explore the deeper meaning of life and seek a higher purpose. A visit to the temple is an enriching and fulfilling experience that leaves a lasting impact on the mind and soul.

In recent years, the Kaal Bhairav Temple has also become a popular destination for spiritual tourism. People from all over the world visit the temple to seek blessings, perform rituals, and learn about the ancient wisdom of India. The temple authorities have taken steps to cater to the needs of these visitors and provide them with a comfortable and safe environment.

The temple also provides various services, such as astrology, palmistry, and horoscope reading, to help visitors gain insights into their future and make informed decisions. The temple authorities also organize spiritual retreats and meditation programs to help visitors connect with their inner self and find peace and tranquility.

The Kaal Bhairav Temple is a destination that offers visitors a unique blend of ancient wisdom, spirituality, and modern-day amenities. It is a place where visitors can learn about the timeless principles of India's spiritual heritage and find solutions to the challenges of modern-day life. In conclusion, the Kaal Bhairav Temple in Varanasi is a destination that offers visitors a transformative experience that leaves a lasting impact on the mind and soul. It is a destination that connects visitors with the timeless wisdom of India's spiritual heritage and inspires them to seek a better future. A visit to the temple is a journey of self-discovery and spiritual enlightenment that is not to be missed.

The Kaal Bhairav Temple also has a significant impact on the local economy. The influx of tourists and devotees generates revenue for local businesses, such as hotels, restaurants, and shops. The temple also provides employment opportunities to the local population and supports the growth of the tourism industry in the region. The temple authorities have taken steps to ensure that the local community benefits from the tourism activities around the temple. They have initiated several community development projects, such as skill development programs, education initiatives, and healthcare services, to improve the standard of living of the local population.

The Kaal Bhairav Temple is a destination that not only offers visitors a spiritual experience but also has a positive impact on the local community and the region's economy. It is a destination that showcases the best of India's rich cultural heritage and inspires visitors to explore the country's diverse traditions and customs.

In conclusion, the Kaal Bhairav Temple in Varanasi is a destination that offers visitors a unique blend of spirituality, culture, and community development. It is a destination that inspires visitors to explore the deeper meaning of life and seek a higher purpose. A visit to the temple is not only a journey of the mind and soul but also an opportunity to contribute to the well-being of the local community and the region's economy.

The Kaal Bhairav Temple is also known for its unique architecture and intricate carvings. The temple has a distinct north Indian style of architecture with a tall shikhara or spire that rises high into the sky. The temple's walls are adorned with intricate carvings of gods, goddesses, and mythical creatures, which showcase the exquisite craftsmanship of the local artisans.

The temple complex also includes several smaller shrines dedicated to various gods and goddesses. These shrines offer visitors a chance to offer their prayers and seek blessings from different deities. The temple authorities have also created facilities for visitors to perform pujas and other rituals within the temple complex.

The Kaal Bhairav Temple is a living embodiment of India's rich cultural and spiritual heritage. It is a destination that offers visitors an opportunity to connect with the divine and explore the deeper meaning of life. The temple's association with tantra, legends, and stories, along with its social and economic impact, make it a must-visit destination for anyone who wishes to explore the cultural and spiritual roots of India.

In conclusion, the Kaal Bhairav Temple in Varanasi is a destination that offers visitors a unique blend of spirituality, culture, architecture, and community development. It is a destination that inspires visitors to explore the deeper meaning of life and seek a higher purpose. A visit to the temple is an enriching and fulfilling experience that leaves a lasting impact on the mind and soul. Visitors to the Kaal Bhairav Temple are also drawn to the vibrant atmosphere and energy of the surrounding city of Varanasi. Known as the spiritual capital of India, Varanasi is a city steeped in tradition and culture. The city is famous for its ghats, or riverfront steps, where pilgrims come to take a dip in the sacred waters of the Ganges River and perform prayers and rituals. Varanasi is also known for its bustling bazaars, where visitors can shop for traditional handicrafts, fabrics, and souvenirs. The city's cuisine is also a big draw, with a wide range of local delicacies and street food available to visitors.

A visit to the Kaal Bhairav Temple is not complete without exploring the rich cultural heritage of Varanasi. Visitors can take a boat ride along the river Ganges, witness the evening aarti ceremony at the ghats, and explore the city's many temples and shrines.

In conclusion, the Kaal Bhairav Temple in Varanasi is not just a destination in itself but is part of a larger cultural and spiritual landscape. A visit to the temple is an opportunity to explore the city's rich cultural heritage, architecture, and cuisine. It is an experience that offers visitors a chance to connect with the divine and explore the deeper meaning of life.

Moreover, the Kaal Bhairav Temple is also a place of learning and knowledge. The temple authorities organize several cultural and educational programs for visitors and the local community, such as lectures, workshops, and seminars. These programs focus on a wide range of topics, including spirituality, mythology, history, and art.

The temple's library is another important resource for visitors and scholars who wish to explore the deeper aspects of Hinduism and Indian culture. The library houses a vast collection of books, manuscripts, and rare texts on various subjects related to Hinduism and spirituality.

The Kaal Bhairav Temple is also a hub for social and community activities. The temple authorities organize several community development programs, such as health camps, vocational training, and educational initiatives, to support the well-being of the local community.

In conclusion, the Kaal Bhairav Temple in Varanasi is not just a place of worship but also a center for learning, knowledge, and community development. It is a destination that offers visitors a chance to explore the deeper aspects of Hinduism and Indian culture, connect with the divine, and contribute to the well-being of the local community.

The Kaal Bhairav Temple is not only significant for Hindus but is also of interest to scholars and researchers studying Indian history, culture, and spirituality. The temple's association with the Kashi Naresh, the former ruler of Varanasi, and its connection to the Tantric tradition make it a subject of research and study.

The temple's annual festival, Kaal Bhairav Ashtami, is a major event that draws thousands of visitors from across India and abroad. The festival is celebrated on the eighth day of the waning moon in the Hindu month of Kartik (October-November) and is marked by elaborate rituals, processions, and cultural programs. During the festival, the temple comes alive with the sounds of devotional music, dance, and chanting, creating an atmosphere of festivity and devotion. The festival is also an opportunity for visitors to experience the rich cultural heritage of Varanasi and witness the devotion and faith of the local community.

In conclusion, the Kaal Bhairav Temple in Varanasi is a destination that offers visitors a chance to explore the deeper aspects of Hinduism and Indian culture, connect with the divine, and contribute to the well-being of the local community. The temple's unique architecture, intricate carvings, association with tantra, and social and cultural impact make it a must-visit destination for anyone interested in spirituality, culture, and history.

Overall, the Kaal Bhairav Temple in Varanasi is a significant destination that showcases the diversity and richness of Indian culture and spirituality. The temple's unique characteristics, such as its association with the Tantric tradition and the Kashi Naresh, its location in the heart of the city, and its social and cultural impact, make it a destination that attracts visitors from across the globe.

A visit to the Kaal Bhairav Temple is an opportunity to connect with the divine, explore the deeper meaning of life, and contribute to the well-being of the local community. Whether it is seeking spiritual enlightenment, exploring the city's rich cultural heritage, or simply enjoying the vibrant atmosphere of Varanasi, the Kaal Bhairav Temple is a destination that has something to offer to every visitor.

In conclusion, a visit to the Kaal Bhairav Temple in Varanasi is an experience that is sure to leave a lasting impression on visitors. It is a destination that showcases the best of Indian culture, spirituality, and community development, and is a must-visit destination for anyone seeking to

explore the deeper meaning of life and connect
with the divine.

Chapter- 4
The recognition of Lord Kaal Bhairav in Hinduism

Lord Kaal Bhairav is a significant deity in the
Hindu religion, particularly in the Shaivism
tradition. He is considered to be an incarnation of
Lord Shiva and is worshipped as the lord of time
and death. In Hinduism, time is considered to be
an aspect of Lord Shiva, and Lord Kaal Bhairav is
believed to be the manifestation of Lord Shiva's
aspect of time.

Lord Kaal Bhairav is often depicted as a fierce and
terrifying deity, with a dark complexion and wild
hair. He is depicted holding a trident and a skull,
and is often accompanied by a black dog, which is
believed to be his vehicle. The dog represents
loyalty and devotion, and is said to protect Lord
Kaal Bhairav's devotees.

Lord Kaal Bhairav is also known as the guardian of
Varanasi, which is considered to be one of the
holiest cities in Hinduism. The Kaal Bhairav Temple
in Varanasi is dedicated to Lord Kaal Bhairav, and
is believed to be one of the most powerful temples
in India. It is said that a visit to the temple can

help one overcome obstacles and achieve success in life.

In Hindu mythology, Lord Kaal Bhairav is also associated with the Tantric tradition, which is a mystical form of Hinduism that focuses on the attainment of spiritual power through various rituals and practices. Lord Kaal Bhairav is believed to be the deity who bestows Tantric powers to his devotees.

In conclusion, Lord Kaal Bhairav is a significant deity in the Hindu religion, particularly in the Shaivism tradition. He is worshipped as the lord of time and death, and is associated with the Tantric tradition. The Kaal Bhairav Temple in Varanasi is dedicated to Lord Kaal Bhairav, and is believed to be one of the most powerful temples in India.

Lord Kaal Bhairav's recognition in Hinduism is not limited to the Shaivism tradition or the Tantric tradition alone. He is also revered in other traditions of Hinduism, such as the Shakta tradition, which worships the Divine Mother in her various forms. In this tradition, Lord Kaal Bhairav is seen as a protector of the Divine Mother and her devotees.

Furthermore, Lord Kaal Bhairav is believed to be an embodiment of the qualities of loyalty, devotion, and protection. His association with the black dog as his vehicle symbolizes his devotion and loyalty towards his devotees. His fierce and terrifying appearance represents his protective nature towards his devotees, and his ability to destroy negativity and obstacles in their path. Lord Kaal Bhairav is also worshipped during the festival of Navratri, which is a nine-day long festival that celebrates the Divine Mother in her various forms. On the eighth day of Navratri, known as Ashtami, Lord Kaal Bhairav is worshipped along with the Divine Mother as a protector and benefactor.

In conclusion, Lord Kaal Bhairav's recognition in Hinduism goes beyond his association with Shaivism and the Tantric tradition. He is revered in other traditions of Hinduism, such as the Shakta tradition, and is worshipped as a protector and benefactor during the festival of Navratri. Lord Kaal Bhairav's qualities of loyalty, devotion, and protection make him a significant deity in Hinduism and a source of inspiration for his devotees.

The worship of Lord Kaal Bhairav is not limited to India alone. It is also popular in Nepal, where he is worshipped as a guardian deity of the city of Kathmandu. The Kaal Bhairav temple in Kathmandu is considered to be one of the most important temples in the city, and devotees from all over Nepal and India visit the temple to seek the blessings of Lord Kaal Bhairav.

In addition to his association with time and death, Lord Kaal Bhairav is also believed to have the power to bestow knowledge and wisdom to his devotees. It is said that worshipping Lord Kaal Bhairav can help one overcome ignorance and gain spiritual knowledge. He is also believed to have the power to cure diseases and protect his devotees from evil spirits and negative energies.

Lord Kaal Bhairav's recognition in Hinduism reflects the diversity and richness of the religion. He is a manifestation of Lord Shiva's aspect of time and is worshipped as a protector, benefactor, and bestower of knowledge and wisdom. His fierce and terrifying appearance represents his protective nature towards his devotees, and his association with the black dog symbolizes his loyalty and devotion towards them. The worship of Lord Kaal Bhairav continues to be an integral part of Hinduism, and his devotees seek his blessings for success, prosperity, and spiritual growth.

There are several legends associated with Lord Kaal Bhairav, which further enhance his significance in Hinduism. According to one such legend, Lord Brahma became arrogant and started misusing his powers. Lord Shiva then created Lord Kaal Bhairav to teach Lord Brahma a lesson and curb his arrogance. Lord Kaal Bhairav is said to have cut off Lord Brahma's fifth head, which symbolized his ego and pride.

Another popular legend associated with Lord Kaal Bhairav is that of the four Bhairavs - Kala Bhairav, Batuk Bhairav, Asitanga Bhairav, and Ruru Bhairav. Each of these Bhairavs represents a specific aspect of Lord Shiva, and devotees worship them for different purposes.

The worship of Lord Kaal Bhairav involves several rituals and offerings. Devotees offer black sesame seeds, flowers, and liquor to Lord Kaal Bhairav as a part of their worship. The Kaal Bhairav temple in Varanasi is particularly famous for its offerings of toddy and meat, which are believed to be Lord Kaal Bhairav's favorite offerings.

In conclusion, the recognition of Lord Kaal Bhairav in Hinduism reflects the diverse and multifaceted nature of the religion. He is worshipped as a protector, benefactor, and bestower of knowledge and wisdom. His fierce and terrifying appearance represents his protective nature towards his devotees, and his association with time and death reflects his power and authority. The worship of Lord Kaal Bhairav involves several rituals and offerings, and his devotees seek his blessings for success, prosperity, and spiritual growth.

Apart from the Kaal Bhairav temple in Varanasi and Kathmandu, there are several other temples dedicated to Lord Kaal Bhairav across India. Some of the popular ones include the Kaal Bhairav temple in Ujjain, Madhya Pradesh, which is considered to be one of the most important Shaivite temples in India, and the Kaal Bhairav temple in Jodhpur, Rajasthan, which is believed to be one of the oldest temples dedicated to Lord Kaal Bhairav.

The worship of Lord Kaal Bhairav is also an important aspect of Tantra, a branch of Hinduism that involves the worship of deities and the use of mantras and rituals to achieve spiritual and material goals. Tantric practitioners often seek the blessings of Lord Kaal Bhairav for protection and to overcome obstacles in their spiritual practices.

In modern times, the worship of Lord Kaal Bhairav continues to be an integral part of Hinduism. His fierce and terrifying appearance continues to evoke awe and reverence among his devotees, and his blessings are sought for success, prosperity, and spiritual growth. The recognition of Lord Kaal Bhairav in Hinduism is a testament to the richness and diversity of the religion, and his devotees continue to seek his blessings with faith and devotion.

In addition to his association with protection and overcoming obstacles, Lord Kaal Bhairav is also considered to be a patron of education and knowledge. It is believed that he is the source of all knowledge and wisdom, and his blessings are sought by students and scholars alike. In some regions of India, the festival of Basant Panchami is celebrated as the day when Lord Kaal Bhairav bestows his blessings upon students and helps them achieve success in their studies.

The worship of Lord Kaal Bhairav also has a significant presence in the Nepalese culture, where he is known as "Kala Bhairava". He is considered to be the protector of the holy city of Kathmandu, and his temple in the city is one of the most important religious sites in Nepal. The temple is believed to have been built during the Malla dynasty in the 17th century, and it is visited by thousands of devotees every year.

In conclusion, the recognition of Lord Kaal Bhairav in Hinduism reflects the multifaceted nature of the religion and the diverse roles that deities play in the lives of devotees. His fierce and terrifying appearance represents his protective nature, and his association with time and death reflects his power and authority. The worship of Lord Kaal Bhairav involves several rituals and offerings, and his blessings are sought for success, prosperity, spiritual growth, and education. His presence in Hinduism and Nepalese culture continues to inspire devotion and reverence among his followers, making him an integral part of the rich and diverse religious heritage of India and Nepal.

The recognition of Lord Kaal Bhairav in Hinduism is not limited to temples and festivals, but also extends to literature and art. The mythological stories and legends associated with Lord Kaal Bhairav have been a subject of inspiration for poets, writers, and artists throughout the ages. The depiction of Lord Kaal Bhairav in Indian art is often depicted as a fierce and terrifying deity, with a sword in one hand and a trident in the other, standing over a demon or a dog, which represents the cycle of life and death.

In literature, Lord Kaal Bhairav is often described as a powerful deity who has the ability to grant boons and fulfill the desires of his devotees. The Kaal Bhairav Ashtakam, a hymn composed by Adi

Shankaracharya, is one of the most popular prayers dedicated to Lord Kaal Bhairav, and it is chanted by his devotees to seek his blessings. The recognition of Lord Kaal Bhairav in Hinduism is a reflection of the vast and diverse religious traditions that exist within the religion. His worship involves various rituals and offerings, and his blessings are sought for different purposes. The worship of Lord Kaal Bhairav continues to inspire devotion and reverence among his followers, and his presence in the religious and cultural landscape of India and Nepal is a testament to his importance in the Hindu pantheon.

The recognition of Lord Kaal Bhairav in Hinduism also highlights the importance of protection and overcoming obstacles in the religion. Lord Kaal Bhairav's fierce and protective nature is a reminder to his devotees that they can overcome any obstacle and challenge that comes their way with his blessings. His association with time and death also reminds them of the transitory nature of life, and the need to focus on the present moment and live life to the fullest.

In conclusion, Lord Kaal Bhairav is an important deity in Hinduism and Nepalese culture. His recognition reflects the multifaceted nature of the religion, and his role as a protector and bestower of blessings is sought by devotees for different purposes. The worship of Lord Kaal Bhairav involves various rituals and offerings, and his presence in literature and art inspires devotion and reverence among his followers. His recognition also serves as a reminder of the importance of protection and overcoming obstacles in life, and the need to live life to the fullest in the present moment.

The worship of Lord Kaal Bhairav is not limited to India and Nepal, but has also spread to other parts of the world with the spread of Hinduism. Hindu temples dedicated to Lord Kaal Bhairav can be found in different parts of the world, including the United States, Canada, the United Kingdom, and other countries with a significant Hindu population.

Moreover, Lord Kaal Bhairav's recognition in Hinduism highlights the diversity and richness of Hindu mythology and the multiple facets of its deities. Lord Kaal Bhairav's association with protection and overcoming obstacles reflects the need to face challenges in life with courage and determination, while his patronage of education and knowledge highlights the importance of intellectual development and growth.

In essence, Lord Kaal Bhairav's recognition in Hinduism and Nepalese culture is a testament to the power and importance of deities in the lives of devotees. His fierce and protective nature inspires devotion and reverence among his followers, while his blessings and grace serve as a source of inspiration and strength to overcome obstacles and achieve success in different aspects of life.

The recognition of Lord Kaal Bhairav in Hinduism and Nepalese culture also serves as a reminder of the rich and diverse cultural heritage of these regions. It highlights the importance of preserving and promoting this heritage for future generations, while also promoting cultural diversity and tolerance among different communities and religions.

Furthermore, the worship of Lord Kaal Bhairav also reflects the importance of community and social harmony in Hinduism and Nepalese culture. Lord Kaal Bhairav's temples and festivals provide a space for devotees to come together, offer prayers, and celebrate their shared cultural heritage. This promotes a sense of community and belonging among the devotees, and fosters social harmony and unity.

In conclusion, the recognition of Lord Kaal Bhairav in Hinduism and Nepalese culture is a testament to the power and importance of deities in the lives of people, and the diverse and multifaceted nature of religion and culture. It highlights the importance of preserving and promoting cultural heritage, fostering social harmony, and promoting cultural diversity and tolerance. The worship of Lord Kaal Bhairav continues to inspire devotion and reverence among his followers, and serves as a source of strength, guidance, and inspiration for overcoming obstacles and achieving success in different aspects of life.

Moreover, the recognition of Lord Kaal Bhairav in Hinduism also reflects the importance of individual spiritual development and growth. Lord Kaal Bhairav's association with knowledge and education highlights the importance of intellectual development and growth, while his fierce and protective nature inspires devotees to face challenges with courage and determination. The worship of Lord Kaal Bhairav thus serves as a reminder of the need to pursue spiritual development and growth, and to cultivate a strong sense of inner strength and resilience.

Furthermore, the recognition of Lord Kaal Bhairav in Hinduism also highlights the importance of environmental stewardship and sustainability. Lord Kaal Bhairav's association with animals and nature reminds us of the need to respect and protect the natural world, and to live in harmony with the environment. The worship of Lord Kaal Bhairav thus promotes an ethic of environmental responsibility and sustainability, and fosters a deeper appreciation of the interconnectedness of all living beings.

In conclusion, the recognition of Lord Kaal Bhairav in Hinduism and Nepalese culture is a multifaceted and complex phenomenon, reflecting the diverse and rich cultural heritage of these regions, and the importance of deities in the lives of people. The worship of Lord Kaal Bhairav inspires devotion and reverence among his followers, and serves as a source of strength, guidance, and inspiration for overcoming obstacles and achieving success in different aspects of life. It also promotes individual spiritual development, environmental stewardship, and cultural diversity and tolerance, and fosters social harmony and unity among different communities and religions.

Finally, the recognition of Lord Kaal Bhairav in Hinduism and Nepalese culture also underscores the importance of the ongoing dialogue between different cultures and religions. It is a reminder that even as we celebrate our unique cultural and religious heritage, we must also strive to promote mutual understanding and respect among different communities and religions. By recognizing and respecting the diversity of religious and cultural traditions, we can work towards building a more harmonious and peaceful world, where people of all faiths can live together in mutual respect and understanding.

In conclusion, the worship of Lord Kaal Bhairav in Hinduism and Nepalese culture is an important cultural and religious practice that highlights the multifaceted nature of religion and culture, and the importance of preserving and promoting our shared cultural heritage. It inspires devotion and reverence among its followers, and promotes individual spiritual growth, social harmony, environmental stewardship, and cultural diversity and tolerance. As we continue to celebrate and promote our unique cultural and religious traditions, let us also strive to build bridges of mutual understanding and respect among different communities and religions, and work towards creating a more peaceful and harmonious world. It is also important to note that the recognition of Lord Kaal Bhairav in Hinduism and Nepalese culture has evolved over time, and has been influenced by various social, political, and cultural factors. As society changes and evolves, so do the cultural and religious practices that shape it. Thus, the recognition of Lord Kaal Bhairav has been shaped by centuries of cultural and religious evolution, and reflects the ongoing dynamic relationship between culture, religion, and society. Furthermore, the recognition of Lord Kaal Bhairav in Hinduism and Nepalese culture is not unique to these regions alone. Similar deities and religious practices can be found in other cultures and religions around the world. Thus, the worship of Lord Kaal Bhairav serves as a reminder of the universality of religious and cultural traditions, and the importance of recognizing and celebrating our shared cultural heritage.

In summary, the recognition of Lord Kaal Bhairav in Hinduism and Nepalese culture is a multifaceted and complex phenomenon that reflects the diverse and rich cultural heritage of these regions. It inspires devotion and reverence among its followers, and promotes individual spiritual growth, social harmony, environmental stewardship, and cultural diversity and tolerance. As we continue to celebrate and promote our unique cultural and religious traditions, let us also strive to build bridges of mutual understanding and respect among different communities and religions, and work towards creating a more peaceful and harmonious world.

Moreover, the recognition of Lord Kaal Bhairav also highlights the importance of mythology and symbolism in religious and cultural traditions. The stories and symbols associated with Lord Kaal Bhairav are deeply embedded in the cultural and religious consciousness of the people who worship him. They serve as a means of transmitting important values, beliefs, and cultural norms from one generation to the next. By preserving and promoting these stories and symbols, we can ensure that our cultural and religious traditions remain alive and relevant, even in the face of social and cultural change.

Finally, the recognition of Lord Kaal Bhairav also reminds us of the importance of spiritual practices in our daily lives. Whether through prayer, meditation, or other forms of spiritual practice, the worship of Lord Kaal Bhairav encourages us to connect with something greater than ourselves, and to cultivate a sense of inner peace and harmony. In doing so, it can help us to navigate the challenges and uncertainties of our daily lives, and to find meaning and purpose in the world around us.

In conclusion, the recognition of Lord Kaal Bhairav in Hinduism and Nepalese culture is a complex and multifaceted phenomenon that reflects the rich cultural and religious heritage of these regions. It inspires devotion and reverence among its followers, promotes cultural diversity and tolerance, and highlights the importance of mythology, symbolism, and spiritual practices in our daily lives. As we continue to celebrate and promote our cultural and religious traditions, let us also strive to build bridges of mutual understanding and respect among different communities and religions, and work towards creating a more peaceful and harmonious world. The recognition of Lord Kaal Bhairav in Hinduism and Nepalese culture also highlights the importance of sacred spaces and pilgrimage sites in religious traditions. The Kaal Bhairav temple in Varanasi is one such sacred site, where devotees come to offer prayers, seek blessings, and connect with the divine. These sacred spaces serve as a physical manifestation of the spiritual realm, and provide a tangible reminder of the importance of spiritual practice in our daily lives.

Furthermore, the recognition of Lord Kaal Bhairav also reflects the importance of balance and harmony in religious and cultural traditions. Lord

Kaal Bhairav is associated with both destruction and creation, and represents the cyclical nature of life and the universe. This recognition of both light and dark, good and evil, is an important reminder that life is a complex and multifaceted experience, and that we must strive to find balance and harmony in all aspects of our lives. Finally, the recognition of Lord Kaal Bhairav serves as a reminder of the interconnectedness of all things. In Hinduism and Nepalese culture, everything in the universe is believed to be connected through a divine energy or force. The recognition of Lord Kaal Bhairav highlights the importance of this interconnectedness, and reminds us that our actions and choices have consequences that can affect not only ourselves, but also the world around us.

In conclusion, the recognition of Lord Kaal Bhairav in Hinduism and Nepalese culture is a complex and multifaceted phenomenon that reflects the rich cultural and religious heritage of these regions. It serves as a reminder of the importance of sacred spaces, balance and harmony, and interconnectedness in religious and cultural traditions. As we continue to celebrate and promote our cultural and religious traditions, let us also strive to deepen our understanding and appreciation of the diverse and complex nature of these traditions, and work towards building a more peaceful and harmonious world.

Whether it is through the recognition of Lord Kaal Bhairav or any other deity, the importance of spirituality and faith cannot be understated in human experience. For many, these beliefs provide a sense of purpose and meaning in life, and serve as a guiding force in decision making and behavior. In a world that often seems chaotic and uncertain, the recognition of a divine presence can provide a sense of comfort and stability.

Furthermore, the recognition of Lord Kaal Bhairav also highlights the importance of cultural preservation and heritage. As we continue to modernize and globalize, it is important that we do not lose sight of the rich cultural and religious traditions that have shaped our societies for generations. These traditions provide a sense of continuity and connection to the past, and allow us to better understand and appreciate the world around us.

In today's world, where globalization and modernization are changing the face of our societies, it is more important than ever to promote intercultural understanding and respect. The recognition of Lord Kaal Bhairav, and the cultural and religious traditions that it represents, is a reminder that our differences should not divide us, but rather unite us in our shared humanity.

In conclusion, the recognition of Lord Kaal Bhairav in Hinduism and Nepalese culture is a powerful testament to the importance of spirituality, cultural heritage, and intercultural understanding in human experience. As we continue to navigate the complexities of our world, let us strive to deepen our appreciation and understanding of the diverse and complex nature of human experience, and work towards building a more peaceful and harmonious world for all.

Whether one is a believer or not, it is important to recognize the role that religion and spirituality have played in shaping human societies and cultures. Throughout history, religion has been a driving force in the formation of cultural norms, moral codes, and social structures. It has provided a framework for understanding the world and our place in it, and has inspired countless acts of charity, kindness, and compassion.

However, it is also important to acknowledge that religion has been used to justify violence, discrimination, and oppression throughout history. It is essential that we recognize and challenge these harmful aspects of religion, while also acknowledging and celebrating the positive contributions it has made to human experience. Ultimately, the recognition of Lord Kaal Bhairav, like any other religious belief, is a personal choice. It is up to each individual to determine what role spirituality and religion will play in their lives. What is important is that we approach these beliefs with an open mind and a willingness to learn and understand.

In conclusion, the recognition of Lord Kaal Bhairav in Hinduism and Nepalese culture is a reflection of the deep spiritual and cultural traditions that have shaped human societies for thousands of years. As we continue to navigate the complexities of our world, let us strive to cultivate greater understanding and appreciation of the diversity of human experience, and work towards building a more peaceful and harmonious world for all.

Furthermore, the recognition of Lord Kaal Bhairav and other deities highlights the importance of cultural diversity and the unique perspectives that different cultures bring to the table. In a globalized world, it is essential that we recognize and celebrate the rich tapestry of human culture, and work towards creating a more inclusive and equitable world that values and respects all cultures and traditions.

In addition, the recognition of Lord Kaal Bhairav can also inspire us to reflect on the deeper meaning and purpose of our own lives. It can serve as a reminder that there is more to life than material wealth and superficial pleasures, and that we must strive to live our lives with a sense of purpose and meaning.

Overall, the recognition of Lord Kaal Bhairav in Hinduism and Nepalese culture offers a powerful message about the importance of spirituality, cultural heritage, and intercultural understanding in human experience. By recognizing and celebrating our differences, and working towards greater understanding and compassion, we can build a more just, peaceful, and harmonious world for all.

Moreover, the recognition of Lord Kaal Bhairav also highlights the importance of respecting nature and the environment. In Hinduism and Nepalese culture, Lord Kaal Bhairav is often associated with the natural elements, such as the earth, water, fire, and air. By recognizing the interconnectedness of all things and the importance of the natural world, we can work towards building a more sustainable and environmentally conscious world.

In conclusion, the recognition of Lord Kaal Bhairav in Hinduism and Nepalese culture offers a wealth of insights into the human experience, and provides a powerful reminder of the importance of spirituality, culture, diversity, and environmental stewardship in our lives. As we continue to navigate the complexities of our world, let us strive to cultivate greater understanding and appreciation of the richness and diversity of human culture, and work towards building a more just, peaceful, and sustainable world for all.

It is worth noting that the recognition of Lord Kaal Bhairav also highlights the importance of spiritual practices and rituals in Hinduism and Nepalese culture. Many people in these communities perform puja or other rituals to Lord Kaal Bhairav to seek blessings and protection. These rituals often involve the lighting of incense, the offering of flowers and food, and the chanting of mantras.

While the practices and rituals may vary across different cultures and traditions, the underlying message remains the same: to connect with a higher power, and to seek guidance and strength in our daily lives. These practices can also help us to cultivate a deeper sense of mindfulness, gratitude, and compassion towards ourselves and others.

In this way, the recognition of Lord Kaal Bhairav serves as a powerful reminder of the importance of spirituality and faith in our lives. It offers a way for us to connect with something greater than ourselves, and to find meaning and purpose in our daily lives. Whether we practice Hinduism or not, the principles of mindfulness, gratitude, and compassion can offer valuable insights into how we can live our lives with greater purpose and meaning.

Finally, it is important to note that the recognition of Lord Kaal Bhairav also emphasizes the importance of community and social cohesion. In Hinduism and Nepalese culture, the celebration of festivals and other religious occasions is often a communal affair, with people coming together to share in the festivities and rituals.

This sense of community and togetherness can help to foster a greater sense of belonging and social connection, which in turn can lead to greater well-being and happiness. By recognizing and celebrating the diversity of our cultural traditions and practices, we can build stronger and more resilient communities, and work towards creating a more inclusive and harmonious society for all.

In conclusion, the recognition of Lord Kaal Bhairav in Hinduism and Nepalese culture offers a wealth of insights into the human experience, and provides valuable lessons for us all. Whether we practice Hinduism or not, the principles of spirituality, culture, diversity, environmental stewardship, and community can offer valuable guidance and inspiration as we navigate the complexities of our world. By working together to build a more just, peaceful, and sustainable world, we can create a brighter future for ourselves and for generations to come.

Ultimately, the recognition of Lord Kaal Bhairav serves as a powerful reminder that we are all interconnected, and that our actions and decisions have a ripple effect that can impact others and the world around us. By embracing the values and principles of Lord Kaal Bhairav, we can work towards creating a more just and sustainable world, one that is guided by compassion, mindfulness, and spiritual connection.

In today's world, where many people are struggling with issues of isolation, loneliness, and mental health, the recognition of Lord Kaal Bhairav can offer a path towards greater well-being and fulfillment. By practicing mindfulness, gratitude, and compassion, we can cultivate a deeper sense of connection with ourselves, with others, and with the world around us. This sense of connection can help to alleviate feelings of loneliness and disconnection, and can promote greater feelings of purpose and meaning in our daily lives.

In short, the recognition of Lord Kaal Bhairav offers a wealth of wisdom and guidance for those seeking to live a more fulfilling and purposeful life. Whether we practice Hinduism or not, we can all benefit from the timeless principles of spirituality, culture, diversity, environmental stewardship, and community that Lord Kaal Bhairav embodies. By embracing these values, we can work towards creating a more just, compassionate, and sustainable world, one that honors the dignity and worth of all beings.

Chapter- 5

Legends and stories associated with the temple

There are several legends and stories associated with the Kaal Bhairav Temple in Varanasi. One popular legend states that Lord Kaal Bhairav was once roaming around the city of Varanasi in the form of a black dog. The local residents were terrified of the dog and asked a Brahmin to perform a puja to get rid of it. The Brahmin did so, and the dog disappeared, but he soon realized that he had made a grave mistake by driving away Lord Kaal Bhairav. The deity was so angry that he appeared in front of the Brahmin and threatened to destroy the city. The Brahmin pleaded for forgiveness and promised to build a temple in Lord Kaal Bhairav's honor. This is said to be how the Kaal Bhairav Temple came to be built.

Another legend associated with the temple states that Lord Shiva once cut off Lord Brahma's fifth head due to his arrogance. As a result, Lord Brahma was cursed with the sin of "brahmahatya" (killing of a Brahmin), and Lord Shiva was cursed with the sin of "bhikshatana" (begging for alms). Lord Shiva roamed the earth as a beggar, searching for a way to rid himself of the curse. He eventually reached Varanasi and visited the Kaal Bhairav Temple, where he was granted salvation by Lord Kaal Bhairav.

There is also a popular belief among locals that Lord Kaal Bhairav is the protector of the city of Varanasi and that he keeps it safe from harm. Many people visit the temple to seek Lord Kaal Bhairav's blessings for protection, especially during times of crisis or danger. The temple is believed to have a powerful aura, and its sanctity is highly revered by devotees.

Additionally, there is a story associated with the nine metallic dogs present in the temple premises. It is said that these dogs were once mischievous boys who played pranks on Lord Kaal Bhairav. As a punishment, the deity turned them into metallic dogs, which were then placed in the temple. It is believed that if a devotee touches the metallic dogs with a pure heart, they will be blessed with good luck and prosperity.

Another popular belief is that Lord Kaal Bhairav is the god of time and oversees the birth and death of every living being. The deity is also believed to control the "kaal chakra" or the cycle of time. Devotees believe that by seeking Lord Kaal Bhairav's blessings, they can avoid untimely death and overcome any obstacles that come their way.

Overall, the Kaal Bhairav Temple holds a significant place in Hindu mythology and is considered a powerful and revered place of worship. Many devotees flock to the temple to seek Lord Kaal Bhairav's blessings and protection, and it is considered a must-visit destination for anyone visiting Varanasi.

Apart from these legends and stories, the temple also has a historical significance. It is believed that the temple was built during the reign of King Bhadrasen, who ruled over Kashi (present-day Varanasi) around 3000 years ago. The temple was later renovated by several rulers, including the Maratha king, Malhar Rao Holkar, and the temple's current form is the result of these renovations. Today, the temple is not just a place of worship but also a cultural landmark. It attracts devotees from all over India and even abroad. The temple is particularly crowded during the festival of Mahashivratri, which is celebrated with great pomp and show in Varanasi.

In addition to Mahashivratri, several other festivals are also celebrated at the Kaal Bhairav Temple, including Navratri, Dussehra, and Diwali. During these festivals, the temple is decorated with lights and flowers, and devotees offer special prayers to Lord Kaal Bhairav.

In conclusion, the Kaal Bhairav Temple in Varanasi is a unique and fascinating place of worship, steeped in history and mythology. It holds a special place in the hearts of devotees and is considered a powerful source of protection and blessings. Anyone visiting Varanasi must visit this temple to witness its grandeur and experience its divine energy.

Apart from being a popular religious site, the temple also has a significant role in the cultural and social life of the city. The temple complex houses a community hall that is used for various social and cultural events, such as weddings, anniversaries, and religious ceremonies.

Moreover, the temple also provides free food to devotees every day. The practice of serving food, known as Annadanam, is considered a noble deed in Hinduism, and the temple authorities have been continuing this tradition for many years. The food served in the temple is considered to be prasadam , a blessed offering that is believed to have spiritual and healing powers.

The temple's proximity to the river Ganges adds to its spiritual significance. Devotees often take a dip in the holy river before visiting the temple, as it is believed to purify the soul and wash away one's sins.

In recent years, the temple has undergone significant renovations to make it more accessible and comfortable for visitors. The temple complex now has modern facilities such as restrooms, drinking water, and seating arrangements. The temple's administration has also taken several measures to improve the safety and security of visitors.

Overall, the Kaal Bhairav Temple is a unique and fascinating place that attracts people from all walks of life. Whether you are a devout Hindu or a curious tourist, a visit to this temple is sure to be an enriching and memorable experience.

In addition to its religious and cultural significance, the temple also has a historical importance. According to some accounts, the temple is believed to have been constructed during the 17th century by a Maratha warrior named Malhar Rao Holkar. It is said that Malhar Rao Holkar, who was a devotee of Lord Shiva, built the temple in honor of Lord Kaal Bhairav after he received a divine message from the deity in a dream.

Another popular legend associated with the temple is that of the Tantric Baba Gorakhnath. It is said that Baba Gorakhnath, a famous saint and yogi, visited the temple in the 11th century and was so impressed by the deity that he decided to stay there permanently. He is believed to have meditated and performed various rituals at the temple, and his presence is still felt by devotees who visit the temple.

Over the years, the temple has become an integral part of Varanasi's cultural landscape. It is not only a religious site but also a cultural hub where people from different communities come together to celebrate various festivals and events. Some of the important festivals celebrated at the temple include Shivratri, Navratri, and Diwali.

In conclusion, the Kaal Bhairav Temple in Varanasi is a unique and significant place that has played a crucial role in the city's religious, cultural, and social life. Its rich history, fascinating legends, and spiritual significance make it a must-visit destination for anyone interested in exploring India's diverse religious and cultural heritage. Visitors to the Kaal Bhairav Temple can also take part in various spiritual activities such as performing puja, offering prayers, and participating in aarti. The temple also has a sacred pond known as the Kotwal Kund, where devotees can take a dip to purify themselves before entering the temple.

One of the unique features of the temple is the presence of numerous dogs that roam freely within the temple complex. These dogs are considered to be the protectors of the temple and are believed to be manifestations of Lord Kaal Bhairav himself. Devotees often offer food and other offerings to these dogs as a way of seeking the deity's blessings.

The Kaal Bhairav Temple is located in the heart of Varanasi and can be easily reached by taxi or auto-rickshaw. The temple is open throughout the day and welcomes visitors of all faiths. However, it is important to dress appropriately and follow the temple's rules and regulations while visiting.

In conclusion, the Kaal Bhairav Temple in Varanasi is a unique and fascinating place that offers visitors a glimpse into India's rich religious and cultural heritage. Its historical significance, spiritual importance, and cultural diversity make it a must-visit destination for anyone traveling to Varanasi.

Whether you are seeking spiritual guidance, cultural immersion, or simply a unique travel experience, the Kaal Bhairav Temple has something to offer for everyone. It is a place where one can witness the ancient traditions of Hinduism and explore the mysteries of Lord Kaal Bhairav.

The temple's serene and peaceful atmosphere makes it a perfect place for meditation and introspection. The sounds of the temple bells and the chanting of mantras create a sense of tranquility that is hard to find elsewhere. It is a place where one can disconnect from the chaos of everyday life and connect with one's inner self.

Overall, the Kaal Bhairav Temple is a testament to India's rich cultural and religious diversity. Its historical significance, spiritual importance, and cultural diversity make it an essential destination for anyone traveling to Varanasi.

In addition to its religious and cultural significance, the temple also serves as a hub for social gatherings and festivals. Many devotees visit the temple during the festivals of Navratri, Diwali, and Shivratri to offer their prayers and seek blessings from Lord Kaal Bhairav.

Furthermore, the temple also plays an important role in the local economy. The surrounding areas are filled with shops selling religious items, souvenirs, and food stalls offering traditional Indian snacks. The temple attracts tourists from all over the world, generating revenue for the local businesses and providing employment opportunities for the locals.

Overall, the Kaal Bhairav Temple is a must-visit destination for anyone interested in exploring the cultural and religious heritage of India. It offers a unique opportunity to witness the ancient traditions of Hinduism and experience the spiritual essence of Varanasi. Whether you are seeking spiritual enlightenment, cultural immersion, or just a memorable travel experience, the Kaal Bhairav Temple is a place that should not be missed.

In recent years, the temple has undergone significant renovations to ensure its preservation and restoration. The government of Uttar Pradesh has recognized the temple's historical and cultural significance and has allocated funds for its upkeep and maintenance. The renovation has not only improved the aesthetic appeal of the temple but has also enhanced the overall experience for the visitors.

In addition, the temple authorities have implemented several initiatives to promote sustainable and responsible tourism. The temple promotes eco-tourism by encouraging visitors to use public transport, reducing plastic waste, and conserving water. The temple has also taken measures to improve the safety and security of the visitors.

Overall, the Kaal Bhairav Temple is a testimony to the rich cultural heritage and religious diversity of India. It represents the spiritual essence of Varanasi and offers a unique experience to visitors seeking spiritual and cultural enlightenment. The temple's historical significance, cultural importance, and religious significance make it a must-visit destination for anyone traveling to Varanasi.

Furthermore, the temple has also become a hub for cultural and social events. The temple authorities organize various festivals, cultural programs, and charity events throughout the year. These events not only provide a platform for local artists and performers but also promote social cohesion and communal harmony.

One of the most popular festivals celebrated in the Kaal Bhairav Temple is the Kaal Bhairav Ashtami. It falls on the eighth day of the waning moon phase of the Hindu month of Kartik. The festival is celebrated with great fervor and enthusiasm, and devotees from all over India visit the temple to offer their prayers to Lord Kaal Bhairav.

In conclusion, the Kaal Bhairav Temple in Varanasi is not just a religious site but a cultural and historical landmark that symbolizes the rich cultural heritage of India. The temple's significance lies not only in its religious and spiritual importance but also in its historical and cultural value. It is a must-visit destination for anyone seeking spiritual and cultural enlightenment and a glimpse into the rich history and culture of India.

Chapter- 6

Description of the temple architecture and surroundings

The Kaal Bhairav Temple in Varanasi is an architectural marvel that reflects the rich cultural heritage of India. The temple is situated in the heart of the city, near the famous Vishwanath Temple, and is easily accessible by road.

There is only one ancient Kaal Bhairav temple in Varanasi, which is located near the Vishwanath Temple. The temple is believed to be over 350 years old and has been an important pilgrimage site for devotees of Lord Shiva and Kaal Bhairav. The temple's architecture is unique and distinct, with intricate carvings and sculptures adorning its walls and pillars. The temple is constructed in the North Indian style of architecture, with a domed roof and multiple entrances.

As you enter the temple, you are greeted by the statue of Lord Kaal Bhairav, seated on a throne, with his weapons and ornaments beside him. The idol is made of black stone and is an impressive sight to behold.

The temple's surroundings are equally captivating, with a small courtyard and a fountain in the center. The courtyard is surrounded by small shops selling souvenirs and offerings for the devotees. The temple's walls are adorned with paintings and murals depicting the different forms of Lord Shiva, to whom Kaal Bhairav is considered an incarnation.

The temple is situated in a bustling part of the city, surrounded by shops and restaurants, giving it a vibrant and lively atmosphere. The narrow streets leading up to the temple are lined with vendors selling flowers, sweets, and other offerings.

In conclusion, the Kaal Bhairav Temple's architecture and surroundings are a testament to the rich cultural heritage of India. The temple's intricate carvings, sculptures, and paintings are a visual treat for anyone interested in art and architecture, while the bustling surroundings give it a lively and vibrant atmosphere. It is a must-visit destination for anyone seeking spiritual enlightenment and a glimpse into the rich history and culture of India.

The temple complex also houses a few other smaller shrines dedicated to other deities such as Lord Shiva and Maa Durga. Visitors can also find a small market outside the temple complex selling offerings and souvenirs.

The architecture of the Kaal Bhairav temple is unique and impressive. The main temple is made of stone and features intricate carvings and sculptures depicting various mythological stories. The entrance of the temple is adorned with a huge black metal bell that is said to have been gifted by the Peshwas of Pune.

Inside the temple, devotees can see the idol of Lord Kaal Bhairav, which is around 3 feet tall and made of brass. The idol is adorned with garlands of flowers and is surrounded by other smaller idols of Lord Ganesha and Goddess Parvati.

The temple is located in the heart of Varanasi, near the Vishweshwara temple and is easily accessible by road. Visitors can hire a taxi or take a rickshaw to reach the temple.

Overall, the Kaal Bhairav temple is a must-visit for anyone interested in Hindu mythology and spirituality. The temple's unique architecture, rich history, and spiritual significance make it a popular destination for tourists and devotees alike.

Apart from the main temple complex, visitors can also explore the surrounding areas, which offer a glimpse into the rich culture and history of Varanasi. The nearby Vishweshwara temple, also known as the Golden Temple, is another popular attraction in the area.

Visitors can also take a stroll along the ghats of the river Ganges, which are just a short distance away from the temple. The ghats offer a stunning view of the river and the many boats and rituals that take place on its banks.

The temple is also known for its various festivals and celebrations, which attract a large number of visitors. The most important festival celebrated at the temple is the Bhairav Ashtami, which falls in the Hindu month of Kartik (October/November).

During the festival, the temple is decorated with flowers and lights, and a grand procession is taken out, with devotees carrying the idol of Lord Kaal Bhairav on their shoulders. The festival is a lively and colorful affair, with music, dance, and traditional food.

In conclusion, the Kaal Bhairav temple is a significant religious site that attracts devotees and tourists from all over the world. Its unique architecture, rich history, and spiritual significance make it a must-visit destination for anyone traveling to Varanasi.

Visitors to the Kaal Bhairav temple are required to follow certain rules and regulations, including removing their shoes before entering the temple premises, and dressing modestly. Photography is also not allowed inside the temple.

The temple is open to visitors throughout the day, although the best time to visit is during the morning and evening aartis, when devotees gather to offer their prayers and perform various rituals. In addition to its religious significance, the Kaal Bhairav temple is also an architectural masterpiece, with its intricate carvings, intricate sculptures, and unique design. The temple's exterior is adorned with images of various Hindu deities, including Lord Shiva, Lord Ganesha, and Goddess Durga.

The temple's interior is equally impressive, with a large hall dedicated to Lord Kaal Bhairav and smaller shrines dedicated to other deities. The main deity is a black stone idol of Lord Kaal Bhairav, which is said to have been installed by Adi Shankaracharya.

In summary, the Kaal Bhairav temple is a fascinating and important religious site that is steeped in history and tradition. Its unique architecture, stunning surroundings, and spiritual significance make it a must-visit destination for anyone interested in exploring the rich cultural heritage of Varanasi and Hinduism.

The temple also has a large courtyard where devotees can offer their prayers and perform various rituals. The outer walls of the temple are adorned with intricate carvings and sculptures, depicting various Hindu deities and mythological stories. Inside the temple, there is a sanctum sanctorum where the idol of Lord Kaal Bhairav is placed.

The idol of Lord Kaal Bhairav is depicted as a fierce-looking deity with four arms, holding a trident, a drum, a skull, and a sword. The deity is adorned with various ornaments and his face is covered with a cloth. Devotees believe that Lord Kaal Bhairav is the protector of Varanasi and the temple is a symbol of his divine power.

The temple is surrounded by a bustling market, where one can find various shops selling religious items, sweets, and souvenirs. The area around the temple is always bustling with activity, with devotees flocking to the temple throughout the day.

In conclusion, the Kaal Bhairav temple is not only a place of worship but also a significant tourist destination in Varanasi. Its rich history, stunning architecture, and spiritual significance make it a must-visit destination for anyone traveling to Varanasi.

The temple complex also includes smaller shrines dedicated to various deities such as Lord Shiva, Lord Ganesha, and Goddess Durga. The temple architecture is characterized by intricate carvings and sculptures that depict various mythological stories and figures. The main entrance of the temple is adorned with a tall tower, and the interior of the temple features a large courtyard where devotees can gather to offer their prayers and offerings.

The surroundings of the Kaal Bhairav temple are equally mesmerizing, with the nearby Kashi Vishwanath temple, Dashashwamedh Ghat, and Manikarnika Ghat. The temple is situated in the heart of the old city, which is bustling with life and vibrant energy. The streets around the temple are lined with small shops and vendors selling a variety of items, including traditional clothing, handicrafts, and souvenirs.

Overall, the Kaal Bhairav temple is a must-visit for anyone interested in exploring the rich cultural and religious heritage of India. The temple's stunning architecture, fascinating history, and tranquil surroundings make it a unique and unforgettable destination.

Visitors are required to follow certain guidelines and rules while visiting the temple, such as removing their shoes before entering and dressing modestly. Non-Hindu visitors are allowed to enter the temple, but they may not be allowed to enter the inner sanctum where the deity is located.

The temple is open to visitors throughout the year, but the best time to visit is during the Hindu festivals of Navratri and Mahashivratri, when the temple is adorned with colorful decorations and thousands of devotees gather to offer their prayers and seek blessings.

In conclusion, the Kaal Bhairav temple is an important religious site in Hinduism that attracts devotees and visitors from all over the world. Its rich history, fascinating legends, and stunning architecture make it a unique and unforgettable destination that should not be missed.

Whether one is a believer or not, the temple's peaceful and serene atmosphere and stunning surroundings offer a sense of calm and tranquility to all who visit. The temple's location in the heart of the ancient city of Varanasi also offers visitors a glimpse into the rich cultural heritage and traditions of India.

In addition to the temple, visitors can also explore the nearby streets and alleys of Varanasi, which are lined with colorful shops, bustling bazaars, and ancient temples. The city is also home to the famous Ghats of Varanasi, a series of steps leading down to the Ganges River, where visitors can witness daily rituals and ceremonies that have been practiced for thousands of years.

For those seeking a truly unique and spiritual experience, a visit to the Kaal Bhairav temple in Varanasi is an absolute must. Whether one is seeking blessings, inner peace, or simply a deeper understanding of Hinduism and Indian culture, the temple offers something for everyone.

Chapter- 7

Miracles and experiences of devotees at the temple

Devotees from all over India come to visit the Kaal Bhairav temple in Varanasi to seek blessings from the Lord and share their experiences of miracles and divine interventions. Here are some of the experiences shared by the devotees:

Protection from a fatal accident: A devotee was once travelling to Varanasi on his motorcycle when he met with an accident. The accident was so severe that the bike was completely destroyed, but the devotee came out of it unscathed. He attributed his safety to the blessings of Lord Kaal Bhairav and has been a regular visitor to the temple ever since.

Success in business: A businessman who was facing a lot of financial difficulties visited the temple seeking the blessings of the Lord. Within a few days, his business started to pick up and he experienced a sudden surge in profits. He believed that it was due to the grace of Lord Kaal Bhairav. Healing from chronic illness: A devotee suffering from a chronic illness had visited several doctors and specialists without much improvement. After visiting the temple and seeking the blessings of Lord Kaal Bhairav, she experienced a miraculous recovery and was able to resume her normal life. Protection from evil spirits: A family was facing a lot of troubles and disturbances in their home due to the presence of an evil spirit. They visited the temple and offered prayers to Lord Kaal Bhairav. After the visit, the troubles subsided and the family felt protected and at peace.

Success in exams: Many students visit the temple seeking the blessings of Lord Kaal Bhairav to succeed in their exams. Many have reported experiencing better concentration, memory retention, and focus after visiting the temple. These are just a few of the experiences shared by the devotees of the Kaal Bhairav temple. The Lord is believed to be benevolent and compassionate towards his devotees and is said to grant their wishes and protect them from harm.

Another miraculous incident that took place at the Kaal Bhairav Temple involved a devotee who had lost his wallet. He had searched for it everywhere but couldn't find it. After praying to Lord Kaal Bhairav, he found his wallet lying right in front of the temple entrance.

In another instance, a devotee who had been suffering from a chronic illness for years had visited the temple and prayed to Lord Kaal Bhairav with devotion. To his surprise, he found himself completely cured of his illness after leaving the temple.

Many devotees also claim to have had their wishes fulfilled after praying to Lord Kaal Bhairav at the temple. Some have reported getting a job or a promotion, while others have reported finding their life partners or getting their financial issues resolved.

The experiences and miracles that devotees have had at the Kaal Bhairav Temple continue to draw countless visitors to this holy site in Varanasi. The temple is not just a place of worship, but also a symbol of faith, hope, and devotion for millions of people.

Additionally, there are many instances where devotees have experienced the power of Lord Kaal Bhairav. One such instance is of a young boy who was suffering from a severe skin disease. His parents had taken him to various doctors and tried all kinds of treatments, but nothing seemed to work. One day, they decided to visit the Kaal Bhairav temple and offer their prayers. After offering their prayers, they applied the sacred ash (vibhuti) from the temple on the boy's skin. To their amazement, the skin disease disappeared completely within a few days, and the boy was completely cured.

Another story involves a devotee who had lost his job and was struggling to make ends meet. He visited the temple and prayed to Lord Kaal Bhairav for help. Soon after, he received a call for a job interview, and he was offered the job on the spot. The devotee believed that it was the grace of Lord Kaal Bhairav that had helped him secure the job.

These stories and experiences of devotees have made the Kaal Bhairav temple a popular destination for people seeking solace and blessings from Lord Kaal Bhairav. The temple attracts a large number of visitors, especially during the holy month of Kartik (October-November) and on Tuesdays,

which are considered auspicious for worshipping
Lord Kaal Bhairav.

A devotee named Neeraj Sharma shared his
experience of how he was able to find his lost bag
containing important documents with the help of
Lord Kaal Bhairav. Neeraj had lost his bag during
his visit to Varanasi, but after seeking the
blessings of Lord Kaal Bhairav, he was able to
locate his bag at the same place where he had left
it.

Another devotee named Pankaj Gupta shared his
experience of how he was able to overcome his
addiction to alcohol with the blessings of Lord
Kaal Bhairav. Pankaj used to drink heavily and had
been trying to quit for a long time, but it wasn't
until he started visiting the Kaal Bhairav temple
regularly that he was finally able to overcome his
addiction.

A group of devotees from Mumbai shared their
experience of how they were able to complete
their Char Dham Yatra (pilgrimage to four holy
sites in India) smoothly with the blessings of Lord
Kaal Bhairav. The group had faced a number of
obstacles during their journey, but after visiting
the Kaal Bhairav temple in Varanasi and seeking
the blessings of the deity, they were able to

complete their pilgrimage without any further hindrances.

These are just a few of the many experiences shared by devotees who have visited the Kaal Bhairav temple in Varanasi. The temple is known for its spiritual energy and is believed to have the power to grant the wishes of its devotees.

Chapter- 8
The power of Kaal Bhairav mantra and its benefits

काल भैरव बीज मंत्र हैं:

"ॐ ह्रीं बटुकाय आपदुद्धारणाय कुरू कुरू बटुकाय ह्रीं" ||
ॐ ह्रां ह्रीं ह्रों ह्रीं ह्रों क्ष्रं क्षेत्रपालाय कालभैरवाय नमः
||

काल भैरव गायत्री मंत्र है:

ॐ कालाकालाय विद्महे, कालातीताय धीमहि,
तन्नो काल भैरव प्रचोदयात् ||

THIS IS VERY POWERFULL MANTRAS

Kaal Bhairav mantra is a powerful Hindu mantra that is dedicated to Lord Kaal Bhairav, who is believed to be an incarnation of Lord Shiva. This mantra is chanted to seek the blessings of Lord Kaal Bhairav and to overcome obstacles and challenges in life. The mantra is also believed to have protective and healing powers.

The Kaal Bhairav mantra is "Om Kaal Bhairavaya Namaha." It is believed that chanting this mantra with devotion and sincerity can have several benefits, including:

- Overcoming obstacles: Chanting the Kaal Bhairav mantra can help overcome obstacles and challenges in life. It is believed that Lord Kaal Bhairav removes all the obstacles and hurdles that are blocking the path of success.
- Protection: The Kaal Bhairav mantra is also believed to have protective powers. It is said that chanting this mantra regularly can protect a person from negative energies, evil spirits, and black magic.
- Healing: The Kaal Bhairav mantra is also believed to have healing powers. It is said that chanting this mantra can help in curing physical and mental illnesses and bring about overall well-being.
- Spiritual growth: Chanting the Kaal Bhairav mantra with devotion can also help in spiritual growth. It is believed that Lord Kaal

Bhairav is the guardian of time and can help a person transcend time and space and attain spiritual enlightenment.

Overall, the Kaal Bhairav mantra is a powerful tool for overcoming obstacles, achieving success, and attaining spiritual growth. However, it is important to chant this mantra with devotion and sincerity, and to seek the guidance of a qualified spiritual teacher.

- Overcoming fear: Lord Kaal Bhairav is believed to be the destroyer of fear, and chanting the Kaal Bhairav mantra can help in overcoming fear and anxiety. It is said that regular chanting of this mantra can give a person the courage and strength to face difficult situations with confidence.
- Enhancing focus and concentration: Chanting the Kaal Bhairav mantra with a focused mind can help in enhancing concentration and improving focus. This can be beneficial for students, professionals, and anyone who needs to concentrate on a particular task.
- Removing negativity: The Kaal Bhairav mantra is also believed to have the power to remove negativity and bring about positive energy. It is said that chanting this mantra can help in

purifying the mind and creating a positive environment.

- Fulfilling desires: Lord Kaal Bhairav is believed to be the granter of wishes, and chanting the Kaal Bhairav mantra with devotion can help in fulfilling desires and wishes. However, it is important to remember that one should not chant this mantra with selfish intentions, but with the intention of serving the greater good.

In conclusion, the Kaal Bhairav mantra is a powerful mantra that can have several benefits for those who chant it with devotion and sincerity. However, it is important to approach this mantra with respect and seek guidance from a qualified spiritual teacher to ensure that it is chanted in the correct way.

- Resolving legal issues: The Kaal Bhairav mantra is also believed to have the power to resolve legal issues and disputes. It is said that chanting this mantra can help in getting favorable outcomes in legal matters.
- Increasing prosperity: Chanting the Kaal Bhairav mantra with devotion can also help in increasing prosperity and abundance in life. It is believed that Lord Kaal Bhairav is the

keeper of wealth and can bless a person with material prosperity and success.

- Purifying karma: The Kaal Bhairav mantra is also believed to have the power to purify a person's karma and help in spiritual evolution. Chanting this mantra with devotion and sincerity can help in creating positive karma and reducing negative karma.

- Enhancing intuition: Lord Kaal Bhairav is also believed to be the Lord of intuition, and chanting the Kaal Bhairav mantra can help in enhancing intuition and psychic abilities. It is said that regular chanting of this mantra can help a person connect with their inner self and attain spiritual enlightenment.

In summary, the Kaal Bhairav mantra is a powerful tool for spiritual growth, success, and prosperity. It is important to approach this mantra with respect and seek guidance from a qualified spiritual teacher to ensure that it is chanted in the correct way. With regular practice and devotion, the Kaal Bhairav mantra can bring about positive changes in one's life and lead to overall well-being.

- Resolving relationship issues: The Kaal Bhairav mantra is also believed to have the power to resolve relationship issues and conflicts. It is said that chanting this mantra with devotion can help in removing misunderstandings and creating harmony in relationships.

- Increasing self-confidence: Chanting the Kaal Bhairav mantra with devotion can also help in increasing self-confidence and self-esteem. It is believed that Lord Kaal Bhairav can bless a person with the courage and strength to face challenges and overcome obstacles.

- Improving communication skills: The Kaal Bhairav mantra is also believed to have the power to improve communication skills. It is said that chanting this mantra with devotion can help in creating clarity of thought and expression, and improving communication with others.

- Enhancing creativity: Lord Kaal Bhairav is also believed to be the Lord of creativity, and chanting the Kaal Bhairav mantra can help in enhancing creativity and artistic abilities. It is said that regular chanting of this mantra can help in tapping into one's creative potential and bringing forth new ideas and inspiration.

- In conclusion, the Kaal Bhairav mantra is a powerful tool for overall well-being, success, and spiritual growth. It is important to approach this mantra with sincerity and devotion, and to seek guidance from a qualified spiritual teacher to ensure that it is chanted in the correct way. With regular practice, the Kaal Bhairav mantra can bring about positive changes in one's life and help in attaining spiritual enlightenment.
- Healing physical and mental ailments: The Kaal Bhairav mantra is also believed to have the power to heal physical and mental ailments. It is said that chanting this mantra with devotion can help in reducing stress, anxiety, and depression, and promoting overall well-being.
- Protection from negative energies: Lord Kaal Bhairav is also believed to be the protector from negative energies, and chanting the Kaal Bhairav mantra can help in creating a protective shield around oneself. It is said that regular chanting of this mantra can help in warding off evil spirits and negative energies.
- Removing obstacles: The Kaal Bhairav mantra is also believed to have the power to remove

obstacles and challenges in life. It is said that chanting this mantra with devotion can help in overcoming hurdles and achieving success in life.

- Attaining spiritual liberation: Lord Kaal Bhairav is believed to be the ultimate guide to spiritual liberation, and chanting the Kaal Bhairav mantra with devotion can help in attaining liberation from the cycle of birth and death. It is said that regular chanting of this mantra can help a person connect with the divine and attain spiritual enlightenment.

In summary, the Kaal Bhairav mantra is a powerful tool for overall well-being, success, and spiritual growth. It is important to approach this mantra with sincerity and devotion, and to seek guidance from a qualified spiritual teacher to ensure that it is chanted in the correct way. With regular practice, the Kaal Bhairav mantra can bring about positive changes in one's life and help in attaining spiritual liberation.

- Cultivating inner strength: The Kaal Bhairav mantra is believed to help in cultivating inner strength and resilience. Chanting this mantra with devotion can help in building mental and emotional strength, and the ability to face challenges with courage and determination.

- Balancing energy centers: The Kaal Bhairav mantra is also believed to have the power to balance the energy centers in the body. Chanting this mantra with devotion can help in activating the chakras and bringing about a state of balance and harmony.
- Improving focus and concentration: Lord Kaal Bhairav is believed to be the Lord of focus and concentration, and chanting the Kaal Bhairav mantra can help in improving mental clarity and focus. It is said that regular chanting of this mantra can help in enhancing productivity and achieving success in one's endeavors.
- Enhancing spiritual awareness: Chanting the Kaal Bhairav mantra with devotion can help in enhancing spiritual awareness and awakening. It is believed that Lord Kaal Bhairav can help in removing the veil of ignorance and guiding a person towards spiritual enlightenment.
- Bringing peace and harmony: The Kaal Bhairav mantra is also believed to have the power to bring about peace and harmony in one's life. Chanting this mantra with devotion can help in creating a sense of inner peace and harmony, and promoting positive relationships with others.

In conclusion, the Kaal Bhairav mantra is a powerful tool for overall well-being, success, and spiritual growth. It is important to approach this mantra with sincerity and devotion, and to seek guidance from a qualified spiritual teacher to ensure that it is chanted in the correct way. With regular practice, the Kaal Bhairav mantra can bring about positive changes in one's life and help in attaining spiritual enlightenment and inner peace.

- Overcoming fear and anxiety: Chanting the Kaal Bhairav mantra with devotion can help in overcoming fear and anxiety. It is believed that Lord Kaal Bhairav can provide the strength and courage to face one's fears and overcome them.
- Purifying the mind and body: The Kaal Bhairav mantra is believed to have the power to purify the mind and body. Chanting this mantra with devotion can help in removing negative thoughts and emotions, and promoting physical and mental purification.
- Increasing intuition and psychic abilities: Lord Kaal Bhairav is also believed to be the Lord of intuition and psychic abilities. Chanting the Kaal Bhairav mantra with

devotion can help in developing these abilities and tapping into one's inner wisdom.

- Manifesting desires: The Kaal Bhairav mantra is also believed to have the power to manifest one's desires. Chanting this mantra with devotion can help in aligning one's energy with the energy of the universe, and attracting positive outcomes.

- Achieving spiritual ascension: Chanting the Kaal Bhairav mantra with devotion can help in achieving spiritual ascension and reaching a higher state of consciousness. It is believed that Lord Kaal Bhairav can help in guiding a person towards ultimate spiritual liberation.

with sincerity and devotion, and to seek guidance from a qualified spiritual teacher to ensure that it is chanted in the correct way. With regular practice, the Kaal Bhairav mantra can bring about positive changes in one's life and help in achieving spiritual enlightenment and inner peace.

- Cultivating self-awareness: The Kaal Bhairav mantra can also help in cultivating self-awareness and self-realization. Chanting this mantra with devotion can help in understanding one's true nature and purpose in life.

- Strengthening one's connection with the divine: The Kaal Bhairav mantra can help in strengthening one's connection with the divine. Chanting this mantra with devotion can help in experiencing the presence of the divine and feeling a sense of oneness with the universe.
- Enhancing creativity: Lord Kaal Bhairav is also believed to be the Lord of creativity, and chanting the Kaal Bhairav mantra can help in enhancing one's creativity and innovation.
- Developing inner peace: The Kaal Bhairav mantra can help in developing a sense of inner peace and calmness. Chanting this mantra with devotion can help in letting go of negative thoughts and emotions, and promoting a state of inner tranquility.
- Improving relationships: The Kaal Bhairav mantra can also help in improving relationships with others. Chanting this mantra with devotion can help in promoting empathy, compassion, and understanding towards others.

In summary, the Kaal Bhairav mantra is a powerful tool for spiritual growth and overall well-being. It is important to approach this mantra with sincerity and devotion, and to seek guidance from a qualified spiritual teacher to ensure that it is chanted in the correct way. With regular practice, the Kaal Bhairav mantra can bring about positive changes in one's life and help in achieving spiritual enlightenment, inner peace, and success in all aspects of life.

- Promoting positive transformation: The Kaal Bhairav mantra is believed to have the power to bring about positive transformation in one's life. Chanting this mantra with devotion can help in letting go of old patterns and habits, and promoting positive changes.
- Healing: The Kaal Bhairav mantra can also be used for healing purposes. Chanting this mantra with devotion can help in promoting physical, mental, and emotional healing.
- Enhancing personal power: Lord Kaal Bhairav is also believed to be the Lord of personal power. Chanting the Kaal Bhairav mantra with devotion can help in enhancing one's personal power and assertiveness.
- Promoting positive karma: The Kaal Bhairav mantra can help in promoting positive karma and attracting positive experiences in life. Chanting this mantra with devotion can help

in aligning one's energy with the energy of the universe, and attracting positive outcomes.

- Offering protection: The Kaal Bhairav mantra is also believed to offer protection from negative energies and entities. Chanting this mantra with devotion can help in creating a protective shield around oneself.

In conclusion, the Kaal Bhairav mantra is a powerful tool for spiritual growth, personal development, and overall well-being. It is important to approach this mantra with sincerity and devotion, and to seek guidance from a qualified spiritual teacher to ensure that it is chanted in the correct way. With regular practice, the Kaal Bhairav mantra can bring about positive changes in one's life and help in achieving spiritual enlightenment, inner peace, and success in all aspects of life.

Chapter- 9

Rituals and customs followed during worship at the temple

The rituals and customs followed during worship at the Kaal Bhairav temple may vary depending on the specific temple and the region in which it is located. However, some common practices and customs followed during worship at the Kaal Bhairav temple are:

Dress code: Devotees are expected to dress modestly and cover their heads while visiting the temple.

Offering prayers: Devotees offer prayers to Lord Kaal Bhairav, seek his blessings, and make offerings of flowers, coconut, sweets, and fruits.

Lighting incense and lamps: Lighting incense and lamps is a common practice during worship at the Kaal Bhairav temple. It is believed that this helps in creating a peaceful and sacred atmosphere.

Chanting mantras: Chanting the Kaal Bhairav mantra is an important aspect of worship at the Kaal Bhairav temple. Devotees also chant other mantras and prayers to seek the blessings of Lord Kaal Bhairav.

Abhishekam: Abhishekam, or the ritual of bathing the deity with various offerings, is also performed during worship at the Kaal Bhairav temple.

Reading scriptures: Reading and reciting scriptures is also an important aspect of worship at the Kaal Bhairav temple. Devotees may read from the Bhagavad Gita, the Ramayana, or other holy texts.

Feasting: After the worship, devotees may partake in a communal feast or prasad, which is believed to be blessed by Lord Kaal Bhairav. Observing fasts: Some devotees may observe fasts on certain days of the week or during specific festivals in honor of Lord Kaal Bhairav. Offering of belpatra leaves: Offering belpatra leaves is considered to be auspicious during worship at the Kaal Bhairav temple.

In addition to the above-mentioned customs and rituals, there are some other practices that are followed in some Kaal Bhairav temples. These include:

Performing yagnas: Some Kaal Bhairav temples perform yagnas or fire rituals to appease Lord Kaal Bhairav and seek his blessings.

Offerings of liquor: In some temples, devotees offer liquor to Lord Kaal Bhairav. This is believed to be a way of invoking his fierce nature and seeking his protection.

Animal sacrifice: Although this practice is not widely prevalent, some Kaal Bhairav temples in certain parts of India still perform animal sacrifices as part of the worship rituals.

It is important to note that animal sacrifice is not a necessary or widely accepted practice in the worship of Lord Kaal Bhairav. In fact, many temples have stopped this practice and discourage its use.

In addition to the above practices, many Kaal Bhairav temples also hold special events and festivals throughout the year. These festivals may involve cultural activities, processions, and other rituals to honor Lord Kaal Bhairav and seek his blessings.

It is important to note that the practices and customs followed in the worship of Lord Kaal Bhairav may vary depending on the region, tradition, and cultural context. It is essential to respect these variations and understand the underlying spiritual significance behind each practice.

In addition to visiting Kaal Bhairav temples, devotees can also perform puja and chant the Kaal Bhairav mantra at home. This can be done by setting up a small altar or sacred space, lighting candles and incense, and offering flowers and fruits to the deity. Chanting the Kaal Bhairav mantra with devotion can help in connecting with the divine and invoking the blessings of Lord Kaal Bhairav.

It is also essential to approach the worship of Lord Kaal Bhairav with humility, sincerity, and respect. Devotees should seek guidance from a qualified spiritual teacher and follow the principles of ahimsa (non-violence), compassion, and kindness in their daily lives.

In conclusion, the worship of Lord Kaal Bhairav is a powerful way to connect with the divine and seek spiritual enlightenment, inner peace, and success in all aspects of life. By following the customs and rituals of Kaal Bhairav worship with devotion and sincerity, devotees can experience the transformative power of this ancient tradition and lead a fulfilling and meaningful life.

Moreover, it is believed that the blessings of Lord Kaal Bhairav can help in removing obstacles, protecting from negative energies, and promoting success in various endeavors. The Kaal Bhairav mantra is also believed to have a purifying effect on the mind, body, and soul, and can help in promoting inner peace and harmony.

In addition to the spiritual benefits, the worship of Lord Kaal Bhairav also has social and cultural significance. It helps in fostering a sense of community and cultural identity, and promotes the values of respect, humility, and devotion.

 the worship of Lord Kaal Bhairav is an important aspect of Hindu spirituality, and has been practiced for centuries by millions of devotees. It is a testament to the enduring power of faith and devotion, and the transformative impact it can have on individuals and communities.

Finally, it is important to approach the worship of Lord Kaal Bhairav with a spirit of openness and curiosity. While the practices and rituals may seem unfamiliar or even intimidating at first, they are rooted in a deep spiritual tradition that has evolved over thousands of years.

By learning about the customs and traditions of Kaal Bhairav worship, we can deepen our understanding of Hindu spirituality and develop a greater appreciation for the diversity and richness of our cultural heritage.

In conclusion, the worship of Lord Kaal Bhairav is a powerful way to connect with the divine and seek spiritual enlightenment, inner peace, and success in all aspects of life. By following the customs and rituals of Kaal Bhairav worship with devotion and sincerity, devotees can experience the transformative power of this ancient tradition and lead a fulfilling and meaningful life.

The worship of Lord Kaal Bhairav is a reminder of the impermanence of life and the need to cultivate a deep sense of detachment and surrender to the divine will. It teaches us to embrace the challenges and uncertainties of life with courage and faith, and to trust in the infinite wisdom and compassion of the divine.

Whether we visit a Kaal Bhairav temple or perform puja at home, the worship of Lord Kaal Bhairav can bring us closer to our spiritual essence and help us realize our true potential as human beings. It can help us overcome our fears and insecurities, and inspire us to live a life of purpose and meaning.

In today's fast-paced and materialistic world, the worship of Lord Kaal Bhairav offers us a much-needed refuge from the stresses and pressures of daily life. It reminds us of the importance of cultivating inner peace, compassion, and self-awareness, and of living a life that is guided by spiritual values and principles.

In conclusion, the worship of Lord Kaal Bhairav is an integral part of Hindu spirituality, and has the potential to transform our lives in profound and meaningful ways. By embracing this ancient tradition with an open heart and mind, we can connect with the divine and experience the true power and beauty of our spiritual heritage. Ultimately, the worship of Lord Kaal Bhairav is a call to awaken our consciousness and realize our true identity as divine beings. It is a reminder that we are not separate from the divine, but rather an expression of its infinite love and wisdom.

By cultivating a deep sense of devotion and surrender to the divine, we can transcend our egoic limitations and experience the joy, peace, and fulfillment that comes from living in harmony with the universe.

In conclusion, the worship of Lord Kaal Bhairav is a powerful and transformative spiritual practice that has the potential to enrich our lives in countless ways. Whether we are seeking spiritual enlightenment, inner peace, or success in our worldly endeavors, the blessings of Lord Kaal Bhairav can help us navigate the challenges and uncertainties of life with courage, faith, and grace.

Through the worship of Lord Kaal Bhairav, we can develop a deeper sense of connection with the divine and realize our true potential as spiritual beings. It is a way of acknowledging the profound mystery and beauty of existence, and of embracing the infinite love and wisdom that surrounds us at all times.

In a world that is often characterized by conflict, division, and materialism, the worship of Lord Kaal Bhairav offers us a path of hope, healing, and transformation. It teaches us to cultivate humility, compassion, and devotion, and to live our lives in service to the greater good.

Ultimately, the worship of Lord Kaal Bhairav is a call to awaken our consciousness and realize the true purpose of our existence. It is an invitation to embrace the infinite potential that lies within us all, and to live a life that is guided by the highest spiritual ideals.

In conclusion, the worship of Lord Kaal Bhairav is a timeless spiritual practice that has the power to enrich our lives and transform our world. By embracing this ancient tradition with an open heart and mind, we can connect with the divine and experience the true power and beauty of our spiritual heritage.

May the worship of Lord Kaal Bhairav guide us on our spiritual journey, and help us to cultivate the qualities of humility, devotion, and self-awareness that are essential for our growth and evolution.

May it inspire us to live a life that is guided by spiritual principles, and to contribute to the well-being and upliftment of all beings.

May the blessings of Lord Kaal Bhairav be with us always, and may we always remain steadfast in our commitment to the path of spiritual evolution and self-realization.

Om Namah Shivaya.

Om Namah Shivaya is a powerful mantra that is often chanted during the worship of Lord Kaal Bhairav. It is a sacred invocation that means "I bow to Shiva", and is believed to have the power to purify the mind and awaken the divine consciousness within us.

Chanting this mantra with devotion and sincerity can help us to connect with the divine and experience the transformative power of Lord Kaal Bhairav's blessings. It can help us to overcome our egoic limitations and awaken to the infinite potential that lies within us all.

In addition to chanting mantras, the worship of Lord Kaal Bhairav may also involve the offering of various puja items, such as flowers, incense, and sweets. These offerings are believed to be a way of expressing our gratitude and devotion to the divine, and of inviting Lord Kaal Bhairav's blessings into our lives.

Ultimately, the worship of Lord Kaal Bhairav is a deeply personal and transformative spiritual practice that can help us to realize our true potential and live a life that is guided by spiritual values and principles. By embracing this ancient tradition with an open heart and mind, we can connect with the divine and experience the true power and beauty of our spiritual heritage.

The worship of Lord Kaal Bhairav is not only a way to connect with the divine, but also a way to connect with our inner selves. By cultivating a deep sense of devotion and surrender to the divine, we can transcend our egoic limitations and experience a greater sense of inner peace, joy, and fulfillment.

The teachings of Lord Kaal Bhairav remind us that we are not separate from the divine, but rather an expression of its infinite love and wisdom. They invite us to cultivate a deep sense of humility and surrender, and to embrace the divine presence that surrounds us at all times.

Through the worship of Lord Kaal Bhairav, we can also develop a greater awareness of our spiritual path and purpose. We can gain insight into our true nature and potential, and receive guidance and inspiration for our spiritual growth and evolution.

In conclusion, the worship of Lord Kaal Bhairav is a powerful and transformative spiritual practice that can help us to realize our true potential and live a life that is guided by spiritual values and principles. By embracing this ancient tradition with an open heart and mind, we can connect with the divine and experience the true power and beauty of our spiritual heritage. May Lord Kaal Bhairav's blessings be with us always.

May we always remain steadfast in our devotion to Lord Kaal Bhairav, and may we continue to cultivate the qualities of humility, compassion, and self-awareness that are essential for our spiritual growth and evolution.

May the teachings of Lord Kaal Bhairav inspire us to live a life that is guided by spiritual values and principles, and to contribute to the well-being and upliftment of all beings.

May we always be mindful of the infinite potential that lies within us all, and may we strive to live in harmony with the divine consciousness that animates all of creation.

Om Namah Shivaya.

Om Namah Shivaya. May the powerful and transformative energies of Lord Kaal Bhairav guide us on our spiritual journey, and help us to overcome our egoic limitations and awaken to the infinite potential that lies within us all.

May we always remain humble and receptive to the divine guidance that surrounds us, and may we approach our spiritual practice with sincerity, devotion, and an open heart and mind.

May we always be mindful of the interconnectedness of all beings, and strive to live in harmony with the natural rhythms of the universe.

May the blessings of Lord Kaal Bhairav be with us always, and may we continue to grow and evolve on our spiritual path.

Om Namah Shivaya.

As we continue on our spiritual journey, may we always be mindful of the lessons and teachings of Lord Kaal Bhairav. May we strive to embody the qualities of strength, courage, and fearlessness, and cultivate a deep sense of devotion and surrender to the divine.

May we always be guided by our inner wisdom and intuition, and trust in the path that unfolds before us. May we learn to let go of our attachments and embrace the impermanence of all things, knowing that all is ultimately an expression of the divine.

May we always be mindful of the power and beauty of our spiritual heritage, and continue to honor and celebrate the ancient traditions that have guided us on our journey.

Om Namah Shivaya. May the blessings of Lord Kaal Bhairav be with us always, and may we continue to grow and evolve on our spiritual path towards greater awareness, peace, and fulfillment.

As we deepen our connection with Lord Kaal Bhairav, may we also develop a greater sense of compassion and empathy towards all beings. May we recognize that the divine exists within each and every one of us, and that we are all interconnected in a web of divine consciousness. May we extend our love and kindness to all beings, and work towards creating a world that is guided by spiritual values and principles.

May we also be mindful of our responsibility towards the environment, and strive to live in harmony with nature. May we take steps to reduce our ecological footprint and preserve the natural beauty and diversity of our planet for future generations.

Om Namah Shivaya. May the blessings of Lord Kaal Bhairav continue to guide us on our spiritual journey, and may we always remain steadfast in our devotion and commitment to the divine.

Chapter- 10

The impact of the Kaal Bhairav temple on the local community

The Kaal Bhairav temple is a popular Hindu temple located in various parts of India, dedicated to Lord Bhairava, who is believed to be the fierce form of Lord Shiva. The impact of this temple on the local community can be seen in several ways:

Religious significance: The Kaal Bhairav temple holds immense religious significance for the local community. Many people believe that visiting the temple and offering prayers to Lord Bhairava can help them overcome obstacles, seek protection, and fulfill their desires. Therefore, the temple attracts a large number of devotees who come to seek the blessings of the deity.

Cultural significance: The temple also has cultural significance as it is a part of the local heritage and tradition. The temple's architecture, rituals, and festivals are all deeply rooted in the local culture and are celebrated with great fervor and enthusiasm.

Economic impact: The temple attracts a significant number of visitors, which has a positive impact on the local economy. Local vendors, shopkeepers, and restaurants benefit from the increased tourism, and the temple itself provides employment opportunities to the local community.

Social impact: The temple plays an important role in bringing the community together. People from different backgrounds and social strata come together to celebrate festivals and participate in religious events. This helps in fostering a sense of unity and belonging among the local community.

Philanthropic activities: Many Kaal Bhairav temples also engage in philanthropic activities such as providing food and shelter to the needy, offering education to underprivileged children, and providing healthcare facilities to the local community. These activities have a significant positive impact on the local community.

In conclusion, the Kaal Bhairav temple has a multi-faceted impact on the local community, including religious, cultural, economic, social, and philanthropic aspects.

Preservation of heritage: The Kaal Bhairav temple also contributes to the preservation of local heritage. The temple's architecture and artwork reflect the local style and craftsmanship, and its preservation ensures that the local culture and heritage are passed on to future generations.

Spiritual and mental health: The temple also has a positive impact on the spiritual and mental health of the local community. Visiting the temple, participating in rituals, and chanting prayers can provide a sense of peace, calmness, and positivity to the devotees, helping them cope with stress and anxiety.

Environmental impact: Many Kaal Bhairav temples are located in natural surroundings, such as hills, forests, and rivers. The temple authorities and the local community often take measures to protect the environment and wildlife in the vicinity of the temple, such as planting trees, preventing littering, and conserving water resources.

Tourism promotion: The Kaal Bhairav temple is often included in tourism itineraries, and its popularity among tourists can help promote the local tourism industry. This can lead to the development of infrastructure and facilities for tourists, creating more job opportunities and improving the local economy.

Interfaith harmony: The Kaal Bhairav temple, like many other temples in India, is open to people of all religions and faiths. This promotes interfaith harmony and tolerance, creating a peaceful and inclusive society.

Overall, the Kaal Bhairav temple has a significant impact on the local community, contributing to their religious, cultural, economic, social, and environmental well-being. It also helps in preserving the local heritage and promoting interfaith harmony.

Chapter- 11

Tips for visiting the temple and precautions to take

Visiting a temple can be a spiritual and cultural experience, and it is essential to be respectful and mindful of the local customs and traditions. Here are some tips for visiting the Kaal Bhairav temple and precautions to take:

Dress appropriately: As the temple is a place of worship, it is advisable to dress modestly and conservatively. Avoid wearing revealing or provocative clothes, and dress comfortably as you may have to stand or sit for long periods.

Remove footwear: It is customary to remove your footwear before entering the temple. You can carry a bag to keep your footwear, or use the shoe racks provided outside the temple.

Follow temple rules: Every temple has its own set of rules and regulations, such as restrictions on photography, mobile phones, and food items. Be aware of the temple rules and follow them to avoid offending anyone.

Be respectful: The temple is a sacred place, and it is essential to be respectful towards the deity and the temple authorities. Maintain silence, avoid touching or damaging any idols or structures, and refrain from littering or spitting inside the temple premises.

Seek permission: If you wish to take photographs or videos inside the temple, seek permission from the authorities. Avoid taking pictures of people without their consent.

Don't disturb others: The temple can be crowded, and it is important to be mindful of others. Avoid pushing, shoving, or rushing, and allow others to offer their prayers peacefully.

Stay hydrated: As you may have to stand or sit for long periods, it is advisable to carry a water bottle and stay hydrated.

Follow COVID-19 guidelines: In the current situation, it is important to follow COVID-19 guidelines such as wearing a mask, maintaining social distance, and sanitizing your hands regularly.

By following these tips and taking necessary precautions, you can have a fulfilling and respectful visit to the Kaal Bhairav temple.

Respect the local culture: When visiting a temple in a foreign country, it is important to be respectful of the local culture and customs. Take time to learn about the temple's history and significance, and be open to experiencing new traditions.

Plan ahead: The temple can be busy during peak hours, such as festivals or weekends. Plan your visit accordingly and arrive early to avoid the rush. Also, check the temple timings and schedule beforehand to avoid any inconvenience.

Avoid giving money to beggars: While visiting the temple, you may come across beggars or individuals asking for money. It is advisable not to give money to them, as it can lead to more begging and exploitation.

Take care of your belongings: Be mindful of your belongings and keep them safe. Avoid carrying valuables such as jewelry or large amounts of cash, and keep your bags and pockets closed and secure.

Seek help if needed: If you need any assistance or have any queries, don't hesitate to approach the temple authorities or volunteers. They can guide you with the temple rituals, rules, and local customs.

By following these tips and taking necessary precautions, you can have a safe, respectful, and fulfilling visit to the Kaal Bhairav temple.

Be prepared for long wait times: During festivals or auspicious occasions, the temple can be crowded, and the wait times to offer prayers can be long. Be prepared to wait in queues and have patience. You can also consider visiting the temple during off-peak hours to avoid the rush.

Don't force your beliefs on others: The temple is a place of worship for people of all religions and faiths. Avoid imposing your beliefs on others or engaging in arguments with them. Respect everyone's beliefs and coexist peacefully.

Don't take anything from the temple: It is considered disrespectful and inauspicious to take anything from the temple premises, such as flowers, prasad, or idols. If you want to offer something, you can donate money to the temple or a charitable cause.

Follow the temple exit rules: After offering your prayers, follow the temple exit rules and avoid lingering inside the temple premises. Also, make sure to dispose of any waste properly and keep the temple clean.

By keeping these tips in mind, you can have a respectful and fulfilling visit to the Kaal Bhairav temple while also being mindful of the local customs and traditions.

Consider hiring a guide: If you are unfamiliar with the local language or customs, it can be helpful to hire a guide who can assist you with the temple rituals and provide more information about the temple's history and significance.

Don't offer meat or alcohol: As the Kaal Bhairav temple is a Hindu temple, it is customary not to offer meat or alcohol as part of your prayers. Respect the local customs and avoid carrying or consuming these items inside the temple premises.

Take care of your health: The temple visit can be physically and emotionally exhausting, so make sure to take care of your health and well-being. Carry any necessary medication, eat a light and healthy meal before visiting the temple, and take breaks if needed.

Overall, visiting the Kaal Bhairav temple can be a spiritual and cultural experience that can enrich your knowledge and understanding of the local traditions. By being respectful, mindful, and following the necessary precautions, you can have a safe and fulfilling visit to the temple.

Respect the sanctity of the temple: The Kaal Bhairav temple is a sacred place, and it is important to maintain its sanctity. Avoid engaging in any activities that may disturb the peaceful environment, such as talking loudly or playing music.

Be mindful of the temple's history: The Kaal Bhairav temple has a rich history and significance, and it is important to be mindful of it while visiting. Take time to learn about the temple's past and its role in the local culture and traditions.

Avoid engaging in any illegal or unethical activities: While visiting the temple, avoid engaging in any illegal or unethical activities, such as drug use or theft. Such activities can not only harm you but also tarnish the temple's reputation.

Follow the queue system: When offering prayers at the temple, follow the queue system and wait for your turn. Avoid jumping the queue or pushing others, as it can lead to chaos and conflict.

Respect the temple authorities: The temple authorities work tirelessly to maintain the temple's sanctity and ensure that everyone has a peaceful visit. Respect them and follow their instructions.

By keeping these tips in mind, you can have a respectful and fulfilling visit to the Kaal Bhairav temple while also contributing to the local culture and traditions.

Chapter- 12

Map & Location of Kaal Bhairav

Geographic coordinates: 25°19′04″N 82°58′26″E☐ / ☐25.317645°N 82.973914°E Coordinates: 25°19′04″N 82°58′26″E☐ / ☐25.317645°N 82.973914°E
Pandeypur Rd, Golghar, Naibasti, Varanasi, Uttar Pradesh 221002

Made in the USA
Las Vegas, NV
08 April 2024

88405133R00066